Field Trip!

Farm

Angela Leeper

Heinemann Library
Chicago, Illinois

Customer Service 888-454-2279
Visit our website at www.heinemannlibrary.com

Designed by Kim Kovalick, Heinemann Library; Page layout by Que-Net Media
Printed and bound in China by South China Printing Company Limited.
Photo research by Jill Birschbach

08 07 06 05 04
10 9 8 7 6 5 4 3 2 1

Library of Congress Cataloging-in-Publication Data
Leeper, Angela.
  Farm / Angela Leeper.
       p. cm. – (Field trip!)
Includes index.
Summary: Introduces a typical farm, exploring different kinds of plants and livestock, machinery, and buildings for housing animals and storing crops.
  ISBN 1-4034-5161-3 (HC), 1-4034-5167-2 (Pbk.)
  1. Farms–Juvenile literature. [1. Farms.] I. Title.
  S519.L44 2004
  630–dc22

                                    2003014523

Acknowledgments
The author and publishers are grateful to the following for permission to reproduce copyright material:
p. 4 Craig Mitchelldyer Photography; p. 5 Robert Lifson/Heinemann Library; pp. 6, 7, 8, 12, 13, 14, 17, 18, 20, back cover Greg Williams/Heinemann Library; p. 9 Ralf-Finn Hestoft/Corbis SABA; p. 10 Randy Vaughn-Dotta/AGStockUSA; p. 11 Ariel Skelley/Corbis; p. 15 Karen Wyle/MidWestStock Photos; p. 16 Elder Neville/Corbis SYGMA; p. 19 Rudi von Briel/Heinemann Library; p. 21 Paul A. Souders/Corbis; p. 23 (T-B) Maximilian Stock, Ltd./AGStockUSA, Karen Wyle/MidWestStock Photos, Rudi von Briel/Heinemann Library, Greg Williams/Heinemann Library

Cover photograph by Greg Williams/Heinemann Library

Every effort has been made to contact copyright holders of any material reproduced in this book. Any omissions will be rectified in subsequent printings if notice is given to the publisher.

Special thanks to our advisory panel for their help in the preparation of this book:
Alice Bethke   Malena Bisanti-Wall   Ellen Dolmetsch, MLS
Library Consultant   Media Specialist   Tower Hill School
Palo Alto, California   American Heritage Academy   Wilmington, Delaware
                                Canton, Georgia

Special thanks to Ganyard Hill Farm and Kooistra Farms, Woodstock, Illinois; Harvard Egg Farm, Harvard, Illinois; and Barb McCarthy.

Contents

Some words are shown in bold, **like this.**
You can find them in the picture glossary on page 23.

Where Does Our Food Come From?

We eat many different kinds of foods.

We eat fruits and vegetables.

We also eat meat and **milk products.**

These foods come from farms.

What Is a Farm?

Farms grow plants for food.

These plants are called crops.

Farms have animals, too.

Farmers take care of the farm.

What Kinds of Crops Are There?

Farms grow many kinds of crops.

Some farms grow corn.

Farmers plant corn in the spring.

They pick the corn in the summer.

What Are Some Other Crops?

pumpkin

Some farms grow pumpkins.

First, pumpkins are green.

In the fall, they turn orange.

You can pick your own pumpkin at some farms.

What Kinds of Animals Are There?

Some farms have cows.

Farmers get up early to feed them.

Some farms have pigs.

They live in pig pens.

What Are Some Other Animals?

Some farms have sheep.

In the spring, a **shearer** cuts off the sheep's wool.

The soft wool comes off in big pieces.

Later, it is used to make clothes.

Are There Any Birds?

Some farms have turkeys.

People eat turkeys at Thanksgiving.

Some farms have chickens, too.

People eat the eggs that hens lay.

What Are the Buildings For?

Farms have many buildings.

Chickens live in a hen house.

silo

barn

Cows and sheep live in a barn.

A tall **silo** holds their food.

Are There Any Machines?

The farmer has many machines to help him.

He pulls the machines with a **tractor**.

Tractors can pull a big wagon.

You may go for a ride!

Farm Map

crops

tractor and wagon

sheep

hen house

pigs

cows

barn

silo

Picture Glossary

milk product
page 5
something made from milk, like
butter and cheese

shearer
page 14
person who cuts off a sheep's wool

silo
page 19
farm building that holds food
for animals

tractor
pages 20, 21
machine that pulls other
farm machines

Note to Parents and Teachers

Reading for information is an important part of a child's literacy development. Learning begins with a question about something. Help children think of themselves as investigators and researchers by encouraging their questions about the world around them. Each chapter in this book begins with a question. Read the question together. Look at the pictures. Talk about what you think the answer might be. Then read the text to find out if your predictions were correct. Think of other questions you could ask about the topic, and discuss where you might find the answers. Assist children in using the picture glossary and the index to practice new vocabulary and research skills.

Index